Successful Psychometric Testing In A Week

Gareth Lewis and Gene Crozier

Gareth Lewis has over 25 years' experience as a consultant in the field of organizational and leadership development. He has worked with a large range of organizations, including many household names, developing HR strategy and systems, and dealing with the management of change.

Gene Crozier has played a key role in the creation of competency frameworks used by public sector organizations as well as blue-chip companies. He has developed a number of psychometric tests and has set up assessment centres for top organizations across Europe.

Successful Psychometric Testing

Gareth Lewis
and
Gene Crozier

Teach® Yourself

IN A WEEK

Hodder Education

338 Euston Road, London NW1 3BH

Hodder Education is an Hachette UK company

First published in UK 1999 by Hodder Education

This edition published 2012

British Library Cataloguing in Publication Data: a catalogue record for this title is available from the British Library.

10 9 8 7 6 5 4 3 2 1

www.hoddereducation.co.uk

Typeset by Cenveo Publisher Services

Printed and bound by CPI Group (UK) Ltd, Croydon, CR0 4YY

Also available in ebook

Contents

Introduction

We can measure how tall someone is, how strong they are or how fast they can run. But is it also possible to evaluate an individual's character traits, how they think and how they might react in a given situation? With psychometric tests, we can.

What is a psychometric test?

If you consider that the term 'psychometric' is formed from the Greek words for mental and measurement, then it's easy to appreciate what these tests do. Quite simply, they measure, accurately and objectively, certain aspects of your mental ability and/or your personality.

Psychometric tests encompass a variety of evaluation tools, which are rather like exams and similarly, in most cases, strictly timed. Some tests are designed to assess your understanding of individual words or a set of instructions; some assess your ability to work with numbers. Others measure whether you can understand relationships between shapes and figures.

There are tests that evaluate your range of critical thinking abilities (deduction, interpretation, etc.) and if you can solve mechanical problems. Tests have also been developed to assess if you are suitable for a particular function or task by measuring, for example, your manual dexterity or hand–eye co-ordination.

Then there are personality tests which can assess everything from a person's motivations and values to their preferred ways of working, their attitudes to authority and their honesty or integrity.

Who uses psychometric tests?

They are being increasingly adopted by employers of all sizes to help them recruit the best job applicants as well as identify the best candidates for promotion among their existing employees. They are quick, inexpensive and, with the right training, relatively easy to administer. They are also seen as a safeguard against possible bias from more subjective forms of assessment, notably job interviews.

In the UK, schools, universities and hospitals are among the wide variety of organizations that use psychometric tests. So do the majority of the biggest and best-known companies in many different industry sectors – automotive, aviation, energy, finance, IT, retail, to name just a few. Other users include the Civil Service, local authorities, the police and the Armed Forces.

How can this guide help me?

Most people feel some trepidation at just the thought of taking a psychometric test. They can also be a source of anxiety for those who have never administered them before. If you are a project manager or HR professional tasked with introducing psychometric tests to your organization and have no previous experience of using them, then reading this book is the first step you should take.

Our aim is to overcome any fear of using tests by demystifying a subject that can for the uninitiated seem quite complex and daunting. This not a technical manual and so we have avoided unnecessary jargon and academic language. You certainly won't need a degree in mathematics or psychology to comprehend any of the contents.

We will provide simple descriptions of psychometric tests, the benefits they offer, and the practical measures you will need to take to use them effectively. In just seven days, you will gain a basic understanding that will serve as a sound foundation for whatever further learning you decide to pursue.

SUNDAY

The importance of psychometric testing

Today we will examine why psychometric testing is important. That it is increasingly seen as important is evidenced by the rapid growth in the use of these tests in recent times.

Organizations now realize that investing in their human assets is essential to their success, but this was not always the case. We will look at how the human-relations approach to management has developed since the 1930s. Employers first adopted psychometric testing to assess the strengths and weaknesses of their people, the results of which would pinpoint an individual's training needs. Then they used testing to help them recruit people with the skills, knowledge and personal attributes relevant to their business or industry.

A factor in the growing popularity of testing was the increasing professionalization of the Human Resources (HR) function. HR professionals, concerned by the shortcomings of the traditional job interview, saw testing as a more objective and reliable selection process. In addition, they considered it a useful aid to the introduction of personal development practices, supporting quality standards such as the Investors in People initiative.

The robust measurement and evaluation offered by psychometric testing would establish it as an effective tool to identify and nurture the key skills or 'competencies' that employers say they need in the modern workplace.

The human-relations approach to management

Since the 1930s and the experiments of Elton Mayo at the Hawthorne Lighting factory, we have seen the development of the human-relations approach to management. We have developed an understanding that the motivation of workers is a key factor in their productivity at work. The importance of human relations as regards the success and productivity of organizations has now been well established, and accordingly the human relations movement has developed and matured. We now take it for granted that investment in people is as important as investment in other aspects of business or organizational life.

What is interesting is that although psychometric testing has been around for much of this century and has been widely available in many forms since the Second World War, it is only in the last few years that the growth has begun to accelerate.

Many of us, particularly in management or senior technical or professional positions, are likely to have encountered psychometric testing in some form. Despite this, there are still many misconceptions about what psychometric tests are and what their potential is in many areas of organizational and personal development.

Environmental influences

What are the influences that have stimulated the growth in testing? The broader influences on organizations include:

- managing change
- competitiveness
- downsizing
- a focus on productivity, and therefore on performance measurement
- a focus on creativity/team-building, and thus on personal behaviour and skills.

As we move through what we have called the human-relations phase, priorities are changing. This is the information age, and along with it is developing the knowledge economy. This will surely see an increase in the importance of the skills, capabilities and knowledge that people hold. In fact, the meaning of the knowledge economy is precisely that the knowledge and skills of individuals and organizations will be tradable; and for many organizations, these factors will be the most important or their only asset.

Any organization in such a position will want to defend its knowledge and skills. But before it can do that, it will need to know what it has got. This will involve an assessment and measurement of things that we have not traditionally been good at assessing and measuring. However, this is where psychometric testing can play a part.

The growth of testing

More specifically, some changes that have had a direct impact on the need for testing include the following:

1 Testing itself has become more sophisticated, with many more tests and suppliers of tests within the market.
2 Increased mobility in the job market, allied to a greater understanding of the cost of making the wrong appointment, has led to a search for more 'intelligent' tools to assess people for recruitment purposes.

3 A substantially greater priority has been given to learning and development in many organizations. This includes a greater need to assess people in terms of strengths, weaknesses and development needs, and psychometric tests have proved useful in doing this.
4 There has been a movement toward assessment as part of performance management.
5 The professionalization of the human-resource function has occurred.
6 An understanding of the importance of personal skills, and of the influence of personal behaviour preferences on these, has also developed.
7 There have been changes in the 'contract' between organization and employee that encompass much more than just the exchange of labour for money.

The development of human-resource practices

Alongside these more general organizational developments, and in healthy organizations at the centre of them, is the Human Resources (HR) function. In parallel with such developments, the HR function has developed many of its practices as part of its contribution to organizational development and success. A number of these are relevant to the present discussion. Some of these include:

● dealing with problems in selection
● quality assurance and development processes
● the movement towards competence.

Dealing with problems in selection

For most of our working lifetimes, the curriculum vitae (CV), along with the interview, has been the stock-in-trade factor in selection. Yet there is a wealth of evidence that this process is flawed. Consider just some of the following points. It has been shown that:

● interviewers make up their mind about a candidate from first impressions and then seek to justify that judgement

- judgements are often based on less-than-rational grounds – such as appearance, gender, accent, etc.
- few interviewers have appropriate training or skills for the job
- even well-conducted interviews, according to the British Psychological Society, are only 25 per cent better than choosing someone by sticking a pin in a list of candidates.

I'M NOT SURE ABOUT THIS ONE...

So what we see is a collection of first impressions, negative information, self-delusion on the part of interviewers and a susceptibility to stereotypes. All of these limitations stem from the fact that the data is entirely subjective.

Once it is recognized that such selection processes are flawed, HR professionals need to identify more rational and effective ways to carry them out. Not least of the reasons for doing this is the cost of getting it wrong. Many costing exercises have been done, and of course the costs involved differ according to many of the circumstances involved. However, for a senior position it is not at all difficult to calculate that a poor appointment can cost upwards of £150,000 when the indirect as well as the direct costs are taken into account. This means quite clearly that it is massively cheaper to do it right first time – even if the direct and immediate costs are higher.

Psychometric testing has an important role to play in good selection procedures. Of course, it is not the whole answer, but tests have a great deal to contribute to robust and effective repertoires of assessment procedures. We shall discuss this in more detail on Thursday.

Quality-assurance and development processes

Training has always been important to most organizations. But more recently, we have seen a broader appreciation of the wider development perspective, and the need to see this as a process. This helps to ensure that development transfers to the working environment and that individual and team development are aligned with business priorities.

This approach is well exemplified in the Investors in People (IIP) initiative. This is a quality standard that underwrites the effectiveness of the development processes within an organization. Although, of course, not all organizations have 'signed up' to IIP, it has been very influential in spreading the word about robust approaches to development.

The model of the process it espouses is as shown in the following diagram:

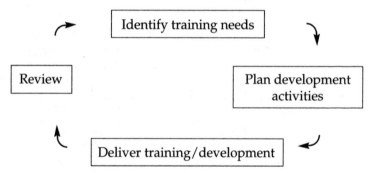

The Investors in People training model

You can recognize this as a typical quality process. However, one of the effects of the widespread knowledge and use of such a model is an increasing focus not just on getting the training done but also on making it 'intelligent'. By that we mean that development activities should be based on a thorough understanding of individual needs.

The knock-on consequence of this is that people need good information in order to understand and articulate development needs. This, in turn, puts the emphasis on means of assessment – everything from performance to ability to behavioural preferences – which is exactly where psychometric tests can often help.

The movement to competence

Organizations are increasingly using the notion of 'competence' as a language to describe the skills that underwrite their organizational development. In fact, there are two separate but related terms to consider here: competences and 'competencies'. Competences are output based and are 'can do' descriptions of the roles and tasks required in doing a particular job effectively. Competencies are more 'to have' descriptions of the fluid intelligences and their associated behaviour. They are the input side of the equation and represent the underlying capabilities and characteristics that enable us to deliver on the competences.

People are our greatest asset

By way of a summary, we can extract from much of the reasoning and evidence above the simple statement:

'People are our greatest asset.'

What we value most about people at work is the knowledge and skills that they apply to that work. As we have said above, there is an increasing focus on the competencies that help people to deliver at work. These are sometimes explicitly called competencies, but they are also referred to as personal effectiveness. Some of the 'core' skills of personal effectiveness which seem to be most sought after include:

- teamworking
- leadership
- interpersonal skills
- management skills
- managing change
- customer skills
- managing self
- lifelong learning and development.

The competence approach, particularly when the focus is on competencies, lends itself very well to measurement and evaluation. And as we have already pointed out, to assess and measure is one of the main drivers of interest in psychometric testing.

Summary

SUNDAY

MONDAY

TUESDAY

WEDNESDAY

THURSDAY

FRIDAY

SATURDAY

We have learned today that major changes in the environment in which organizations operate – such as growing competition, downsizing and a greater focus on productivity – are forcing them to make further substantial changes internally in order to remain competitive and profitable.

Many of the main HR practices have become more professional and sophisticated as a result of those pressures. The direct and indirect costs of making the wrong appointment or promotion are prohibitive, which no employer can afford even at the best of times. This has involved a higher level of scrutiny on how we recruit, retain, manage and develop staff. With impressions gained from interviews being entirely subjective, testing can make assessment procedures more robust and effective.

We have described the major trends that have led to increasing importance being attached to skills of personal effectiveness – or competencies, as we now know to call them – and how assessment and measurement are now seen as the best means of evaluating these. This is why there has been an acceleration in the adoption of psychometric tests in the last two decades, and why this is set to continue in the years to come.

Tomorrow we will take a closer look at the origins of these tests.

Fact-check (answers at the back)

1. How important is investment in people compared to investment in other aspects of business or organizational life?
   a) Less important ❏
   b) As important ❏
   c) More important ❏
   d) Not important at all ❏

2. Psychometric testing has been widely available in many forms since when?
   a) The Crimean War ❏
   b) The First World War ❏
   c) The Second World War ❏
   d) The Vietnam War ❏

3. What influences have stimulated the growth in testing?
   a) Managing change ❏
   b) Competitiveness and downsizing ❏
   c) A focus on productivity ❏
   d) A focus on creativity and team-building ❏

4. In which areas have psychometric tests proved useful in assessing people?
   a) Strengths ❏
   b) Weaknesses ❏
   c) Development needs ❏
   d) Driving skills ❏

5. Which areas of modern HR practices are relevant to psychometric testing?
   a) Organizing the staff Christmas party ❏
   b) Dealing with problems in selection ❏
   c) Quality assurance and development processes ❏
   d) The movement towards competence ❏

6. Which of these are limitations of conventional job interviews?
   a) First impressions ❏
   b) Self-delusion on the part of interviewers ❏
   c) Susceptibility to stereotypes ❏
   d) A national shortage of comfortable chairs ❏

7. What is the name of the quality standard that has been very influential in encouraging robust approaches to personal development?
   a) Investors in Professionals ❏
   b) Investors in Practices ❏
   c) Investors in Performance ❏
   d) Investors in People ❏

8. Which of these steps form part of the Investors in People training model?
   a) Identify training needs ❏
   b) Plan development activities ❏
   c) Deliver training/development ❏
   d) Review ❏

9. What are personal effectiveness skills also known as?
   a) Comparators ❏
   b) Competences ❏
   c) Competencies ❏
   d) Compatibilities ❏

10. Which of these is not one of the 'core' skills of personal effectiveness which are sought after by employers?
    a) Teamworking ❏
    b) Leadership ❏
    c) Being good at darts ❏
    d) Interpersonal skills ❏

MONDAY

What are psychometric tests?

There is still widespread confusion as to what exactly makes a test *psychometric*. One popular misconception is that only tests that give us information about an individual's personality or attitudes are, in fact, psychometric. This is not true, for the term can be equally applied to tests that evaluate our ability to perform certain tasks.

So what are the defining characteristics of such a test? Or, to put it another way: what does a test have to be to be called psychometric? In short, it has to measure and quantify attributes – qualities and features that are regarded as a characteristic or inherent part of you. There are also criteria in relation to how a test is administered, scored and interpreted.

In this chapter, we will also introduce you to the term 'items', as the questions in psychometric tests are called, and give you examples of the various forms they take. And when deciding which test to use, we look at the two key issues to consider: validity and reliability.

To tell you what you need to know about these and other issues, today will cover:

● the history of psychometric testing
● what puts the 'psycho' in psychometric
● what puts the 'metric' in psychometric
● interpreting test results.

The history of psychometric testing

It is fairly natural and human to make judgements about the behaviour or potential of other people. This has been done throughout history, and as individuals we probably carry on this tradition ourselves. Just think of those people who may have made judgements about you over the years. Your list might include:

- parents and relatives
- friends
- teachers
- workmates
- managers and potential employers.

However, on the whole, these judgements will most likely have been either subjective or based on flawed or incomplete information.

HE WOULD MAKE A GOOD
PSHYCHOMETRIC TESTER...

The first person to take a more systematic or 'scientific' approach to measuring some aspect of human behaviour or capability was a French psychologist called Alfred Binet. Binet was interested in the differences between children who achieved through education and those who did not, and he sought to be able to identify and measure those differences.

The focus of his interest was on those skills, including judgement, comprehension and ability to reason, which he felt distinguished achievers from non-achievers. He invented the term 'intelligence quotient' (IQ) to describe these characteristics, and he went on to develop a test to measure them objectively. Over the years, and for various reasons, the notion of IQ has been somewhat discredited, but today we are able to measure, by testing, a number of similar or related concepts.

The first major users of such tests were the military in the USA, but since the Second World War psychometric testing has moved both to education and to organizational life in general. The main difference today is that we can now measure a much broader range of characteristics using a comprehensive range of sophisticated instruments.

What puts the 'psycho' in psychometric?

Although there are many definitions, the British Psychological Society describes a psychometric test as: 'an instrument designed to produce a quantitative assessment of some psychological attribute or attributes'. '[S]ome psychological attribute' is a good description, but it doesn't tell us too much!

An alternative definition talks about: '...a capacity, propensity or liability to act, react, experience or to structure or order thought or behaviour in particular ways'.

In general, psychometric tests tend to relate to two distinct (but overlapping) kinds of performance:

1 Maximum performance

Tests here relate to our capacity or capability to do certain things. They include tests of intelligence, aptitude or ability. We will describe the full range of such tests tomorrow. For now, it is worth noting that they typically:

- have right and wrong answers
- measure the ability or achievement under strict conditions
- involve a certain level of difficulty so that performance can be compared from person to person.

2 Habitual performance

This is also sometimes called 'typical performance', and tests here involve attempts to measure characteristic ways of behaving. They can also involve a consideration of how we perceive the world, and of attitudes, values and interests. These tests:

● are self-descriptive
● indicate the most typical behaviour or preferences
● don't involve right or wrong answers.

They are sometimes also referred to as 'psychological tests' or 'personality tests'. Interestingly, it is a common mistake for people to assume that it is just these (rather than the ability tests also) that are 'psychometric'.

We will discuss these tests in much more detail on Wednesday.

What puts the 'metric' in psychometric?

Clearly, as the name implies, this has something to do with measurement. It is primarily the fact that we are measuring and quantifying attributes that distinguishes psychometric testing from subjective judgement. However, developing a test is a whole process, and one which involves a number of components.

So there are a number of criteria that enable us to classify a test as psychometric. These include the following:

● it is constructed according to psychometric principles
● it is administered in a standardized way
● it is scored in a standardized way
● it is interpreted in a standardized way.

How tests are developed

Most tests are of the pencil-and-paper type and consist of questions – or items, as they are called – and the basic process of constructing a test involves:

1 generating a large number of items
2 the piloting and selection of items – this is done on the basis of a number of statistical tests which are described below

3 standardizing the scores – this enables raw scores to be
  translated into comparative scores
4 writing the technical manual.

This process should be available to users of all robust tests,
and should contain information both about the relevant
statistics and about the appropriate administration, scoring
and interpreting of the test.

Items for tests

For ability tests, like tests of intelligence, items can take
various forms. Here are some examples:

● **Analogy**

Sparrow is to bird as minnow is to ...				
a) animal	b) ant	c) fish	d) bird	e) reptile

● **Odd man out**

24	63	10	48	35

● **Sequences**

8	11	14	17	...

For most purposes, items are multi-choice, with only one right
answer. However, there are variations, such as matching items.
  For personality tests, there are a number of possibilities:

● **Dual response:** like 'yes/no' or 'true/false'. A variation on
  this is where a third, interim category is added, e.g.:
  – 'yes/not sure/no'
  – 'mostly/sometimes/never'
  – 'agree/uncertain/false'.
● **Rating scales:** where words on a continuum are each
  associated with a number, e.g.:

Always	often	sometimes	never
1	2	3	4

● **Forced choice:** sometimes called ipsative. Here, subjects
  are forced to choose, usually from a pair of words, which one
  most applies to them.

Selecting and testing items

There are a number of statistical tests that the items and the test as a whole should pass, and we will provide here a brief (and not too technical) overview which should give you an idea of the important considerations and questions to ask.

The two basic concepts that are involved are:

1 validity
2 reliability.

Validity

A test is valid if it measures what it says it measures. This is a simple starting point, but validity can be a complex topic. There are a number of facets to it, and thus a number of different ways of describing, measuring and demonstrating validity. The most important are:

- **face validity:** this is the extent to which the test appears to the user to test the attribute in question. Its main value is in gaining co-operation from test-takers
- **construct validity:** the question here is whether the test fully describes the variable being measured
- **content validity:** this answers the question 'Does this test measure all aspects of the variable in question?'
- **criterion-related validity:** this establishes the predictive value of the test: whether it can predict some measured, real-world criterion. In general, this is quite difficult to

achieve to a high degree. However, where it can be justified, it is obviously very powerful.

Reliability

Reliability has two distinct meanings. A test is reliable if it is self-consistent – that is, its various parts are measuring the same thing. A good test should also give the same score for each subject (as long as their ability has not changed) when they are retested. This is called test–retest reliability.

Reliability is also important in influencing the validity factor: valid tests are also consistent ones.

Whenever you are faced with choices about using tests, you should ask searching questions about the reliability and validity of a test. As a user, you need to be reassured by its robustness and effectiveness.

Administering tests

The results of a test are meaningful and reliable only if everyone takes it in the same conditions. This can be illustrated by a very simple example. Suppose you want to test a group of people using a numerical-ability test. You could just hand the test out and ask the subjects to return it in the next few days. However, there would be a few disadvantages to this:

- they might 'crib' the answers
- they would be doing the test in different conditions and environments
- they would take different amounts of time to do the test.

If any or all of these are the case, then we would not be comparing apples with apples.

In the case of an ability test, the time to answer might be an important part of the variable being measured, which is why many ability tests are timed.

To get over these problems, test suppliers should supply a user manual which describes the test administration in some detail, including the actual script to be spoken.

For the reasons outlined above, it is important that these instructions be kept to precisely.

Interpreting test results

If a subject scores 20 out of 25 on a verbal-reasoning test, what does this mean? A first response might be to say that, because they have scored more than half, that must be a good result. But, on the other hand, doesn't it depend on how 'difficult' the test is?

It is for this reason that raw scores on a test are always converted into a 'profile score' which compares the score for this subject with the scores of some known group of people. This process is called standardizing the scores. It works in the following way.

As with most variables that occur in the natural world, measurements for a population are distributed in a characteristic way. For instance, if we measured the heights of a large and representative sample of the population and put these on a **frequency diagram**, they would look as shown in the figure below.

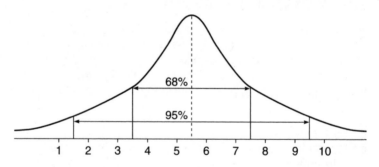

The shape of this line occurs so often that it has been given a name: the 'normal distribution'. It is bell-shaped and symmetrical, and the average (or mean) is the highest point on the curve.

Another statistic which is very relevant in this distribution is called the 'standard deviation' (SD). This is the square root of the average distance of the scores from the mean, and it measures the spread of the distribution. Its main advantage is that we can work out the proportion of people who score above or below any particular standard-deviation score. For instance, we know that 68 per cent of people will score between plus and minus 1 SD score (the area shown on the figure). When raw scores are converted into standardized scores, each score is placed in relation to the rest of the population. There are two popular ways of doing this:

1 **sten (standard ten) scores:** these 'carve' the distribution up into 10 units, with the middle being at 5.5 – see the figure
2 **percentiles:** these carve the distribution up into 100 units, with the middle being at 50.

A question worth asking with the standardized scores used for any test is: what is the group or population against which I am being compared? A percentile score, on an ability test, of 60 (which means a score higher than 60 per cent of the population) is one thing if you are being compared with the population *as a whole*. However, if you are being compared to just a graduate or a senior-management population, then the interpretation will be slightly different.

SUNDAY
MONDAY
TUESDAY
WEDNESDAY
THURSDAY
FRIDAY
SATURDAY

Summary

By now some of you may be feeling that adopting psychometric testing is going to be a lot harder than you thought – but don't be put off by all the jargon!

The 'technical' aspect of test design and interpretation is certainly complex, but while there are some convoluted ideas here, the important things to bear in mind are quite simple:

● The 'science' of testing means not only that tests are systematically designed, but also that there are measures of important aspects of tests that you should ask about and pay attention to – among these, information about reliability and validity are the most critical

● Tests should be administered and scored in a standardized way, according to the publisher's instructions

● Scores are made meaningful by being converted into standardized scores to compare the results with a known group or population; the most common ways to do this are by using sten scores or percentiles.

Finally, of course, in many circumstances we will need to give subjects feedback on their results. However, we will discuss this in more detail on Friday.

SUNDAY
MONDAY
TUESDAY
WEDNESDAY
THURSDAY
FRIDAY
SATURDAY

Fact-check (answers at the back)

1. Psychometric tests tend to relate to which distinct kinds of performance?
   a) Maximum ☐
   b) Minimum ☐
   c) Habitual ☐
   d) Occasional ☐

2. Which of these criteria are used to classify a test as psychometric?
   a) It is folded in a standardized way ☐
   b) It is administered in a standardized way ☐
   c) It is scored in a standardized way ☐
   d) It is interpreted in a standardized way ☐

3. What are test questions better known as?
   a) Things ☐
   b) Items ☐
   c) Elements ☐
   d) Articles ☐

4. Which of these are typical forms of items in ability tests?
   a) Analogy ☐
   b) Odd man out ☐
   c) Pig in a poke ☐
   d) Sequences ☐

5. Which of these are variations of items used in personality tests?
   a) Dual response ☐
   b) Rating scales ☐
   c) Truth or dare ☐
   d) Forced choice ☐

6. Which of these is not a measure of a test's validity?
   a) Face validity ☐
   b) Construct validity ☐
   c) Content validity ☐
   d) Criterion-related validity ☐

7. Along with validity, what is the other important factor to consider when selecting a psychometric test?
   a) Responsiveness ☐
   b) Reputation ☐
   c) Reliability ☐
   d) Realism ☐

8. What is the process of converting raw scores into a profile score called?
   a) Adding up the scores ☐
   b) Profiling the scores ☐
   c) Standardizing the scores ☐
   d) Evening out the scores ☐

9. What is the name of the statistic for the square root of the average distance of the scores from the mean?
   a) The average ☐
   b) The mode ☐
   c) The standard deviation ☐
   d) The X Factor ☐

10. What are two common methods for converting raw scores into standardized scores?
    a) Sten scores ☐
    b) Mean scores ☐
    c) Percentiles ☐
    d) Proportions ☐

Tests of ability and aptitude

Yesterday we made the distinction between tests of maximum performance and tests of habitual or typical performance. It is the former that are the tests of ability and aptitude, and we shall focus on these in more detail today.

First, we shall look at the concept of intelligence – still important to the understanding of psychometric testing more than 100 years after the first IQ tests were developed.

Next, we will cover the various types of test available. These include ones designed to test your verbal, numerical and abstract reasoning, and we will give you some examples of all three. Others will assess your knowledge by testing your mechanical reasoning or critical thinking ability. Some tests have been developed specifically to evaluate whether you are suitable for a particular job or even a single function.

In the final section of this chapter, we will list some guidelines for selecting and using tests. The data produced by a test will be of no use if you have not done the necessary preparatory work to identify if the test is appropriate to your organization's needs. If in doubt, it is always advisable to seek the advice of an expert. So don't be afraid to ask!

The concept of intelligence

We need to consider this topic because, as we have explained, it is at the heart of the development of psychometric testing. Many of the reasons that made it of interest at the turn of the last century are just as valid today. Although the language and the degree of sophistication of the testing process have changed, it is still just as important.

Binet's approach to intelligence, as already mentioned, was expressed in terms of the intelligence quotient (IQ). This expressed the ratio of the mental age to the chronological age and was based around an average of 100. Because it related intelligence to development, and its primary focus was children, the measure was not appropriate when applied to adults. However, the concept was nonetheless considered to be important. Having said that, we also need to understand that it has been remarkably difficult to define the concept without colliding with different cultural definitions as to what constitutes intelligence.

What we do know is that the ability to perform certain types of task successfully means that it is more likely that we can also perform other, similar types of task successfully. Thus, psychologists have postulated such a thing as 'general intelligence'. Intelligence has been described by Spearman as the quality that allows people to do well on most tasks. This is seen as the 'driving force' behind many of the more specific abilities that we recognize and which we can measure. This description does suggest some types of continuum:

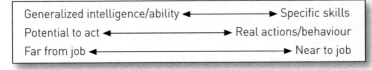

Generalized intelligence/ability ←————————→ Specific skills

Potential to act ←————————→ Real actions/behaviour

Far from job ←————————————→ Near to job

This demonstrates that either we can seek to look at the underlying capability or we can focus on specific skills that are known to be of interest. It is the particular context that will dictate which of these (or both) is of most interest.

Types of test

We have already described that the early history of testing was focused on the generalized notion of intelligence. However, it soon grew from there. The recognition of the complex nature of ability, and of the continuum which moves from the very general to the highly specific, widened out the scope of interest. Any ability that humans can use or express, and any behaviour that they undertake, can in principle be tested for. This means that there is an astonishing range of possible candidates for testing. As a general guide, it is worth following the dictum that anything that can be tested almost certainly has been. In this section, we shall describe and illustrate some of the major categories of test.

Before we look in detail at different types of test, we should note that ability tests do have some characteristics that set them apart from the personality tests that we shall discuss tomorrow. These include:

● they are not self-assessed
● they involve right–wrong answers (with certain exceptions)
● they are administered in rigorous circumstances, particularly in selection and recruitment procedures
● they are often timed.

In general, there are three classes of test:

1 **objective ability tests** – which test general intellectual functions, or more specific abilities
2 **achievement tests** – such as reading, clerical coding and basic operator skills
3 **performance tests** – such as standardized work-sample tests.

General ability tests

These test underlying cognitive ability and mental functioning. Typical of these are tests of verbal and numerical reasoning. Many test suppliers supply tests with both these components, and sometimes a third component, abstract reasoning, is also added. Such collections are called 'batteries' of tests. A battery of tests is a collection of tests that together give a rounded picture of the psychological attributes sought by the tester.

A typical battery is the GRT series by Psytech which provides verbal, numerical and abstract tests at both general and graduate levels. Typical (but not actual) items look like this:

● **Verbal:** designed to test an understanding of words and of relationships between words.

Dark means the opposite of...?					
1	2	3	4	5	6
gloomy	happy	red	heavy	light	day

● **Numeric:** designed to assess the ability to work with numbers.

4 is to 12 as 8 is to?					
1	**2**	**3**	**4**	**5**	**6**
16	24	20	64	32	36

● **Abstract:** designed to assess relationships between shapes and figures.

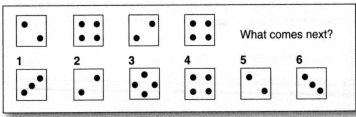

It should also be borne in mind that tests and test batteries should be sensitized to the level of the takers. In this way, the AH series of tests is differentiated by ability. AH4, 3 and 2 are suitable for the general population, while AH5 and 6 are suitable for a graduate population.

The Raven Progressive Matrices is another well-known test which exists in standard and advanced versions.

Other ability tests

Some tests involve knowledge or achievement as well as ability. Examples might include tests of:

● mechanical reasoning or mechanical comprehension
● critical thinking ability.

An example of the above is the Watson-Glaser Critical Thinking Appraisal. This tests for a range of critical reasoning abilities such as:

● the ability to draw inferences
● the recognition of assumptions
● deduction
● interpretation
● the evaluation of arguments.

For example:

> **Statement:**
> Some holidays are rainy. All rainy days are boring.
>
> **Therefore:**
> Proposed conclusions (Yes/No)
> 1 No clear days are boring
> 2 Some holidays are boring
> 3 Some holidays are not boring

Occupational ability tests

Even more specific in their analysis of abilities, these tests have been developed for particular jobs or quite specific applications. Examples include tests for:

- programming
- computer operations
- word processing
- foreign-language learning
- clerical aptitude
- manual dexterity
- hand–eye co-ordination.

Skills and knowledge tests

These can take a number of forms. They can be targeted at basic skills such as reading, arithmetic, oral communication and so on. Alternatively, they can be targeted at more specific job-related skill areas such as clerical, typing and other operator skills. Where they are related to a knowledge base, they typically seek not just knowledge of facts but also ability to make judgements and make decisions when using the knowledge base.

An example of an applied judgement test is the Management Self Assessment Test (MSAT) developed by the Chartered Management Institute. This is a self-assessment test which covers important elements of required managerial knowledge and judgement. Thus, it gives an indication of the level of performance in a management role. It looks at:

- general managerial knowledge and judgement
- the ability to conceptualize typical management problems and solutions
- the ability to think critically and logically in solving those problems.

It involves 70 questions based on seven realistic management scenarios or case studies. Here is a sample item:

---

1. In Arab countries during Ramadan, good Muslims do not eat during the day but only after sundown and before sunrise. An expatriate Western manager has found it commercially profitable to give key account clients a buffet lunch when making marketing presentations. During Ramadan, what should he do?

   a) skip the food
   b) have food in another room for non-Muslims
   c) give the presentation and lunch in the evening
   d) make no change in his routine

What is involved in developing skills and knowledge tests? Developing job-specific tests may be attractive, but just what is involved and how much does it cost? To develop MSAT, the Chartered Management Institute needed to satisfy three requirements:

1 possession of specialist expertise in test design and validation
2 access to a group of subject-matter experts
3 the opportunity to test the items on a representative sample of managers.

The test itself was designed over a period of six months using about 20 subject-matter experts. Most of the time was taken up reviewing and editing items. In this first stage, a pool of managers from different organizations was used to review and test the individual items. Once the test had been designed, field trials were carried out to prove the test worked. The test was applied to over 1,500 managers in a variety of organizations. Some items which had appeared OK in the early trials soon revealed problems, and the test had to be adjusted. Once the final format for the test had been decided, samples had to be analysed to demonstrate the link between the test results and job performance (in this case, the level of management). This stage took more than six months.

All this took slightly more than one year to complete. In staff terms, it required a significant commitment from one senior manager, specialist expertise from one occupational psychologist and support from a significant number of companies.

Job performance tests

Performance tests have been developed for many craft and technical jobs. As well as current ability, they can also focus on the ability to learn in real work situations.

Guidelines for selecting and using tests

In this section, we shall gather some thoughts about how to use ability tests in practice.

1 **Start with the job.** As always with assessment exercises, it is necessary to have a detailed description of the required skills. The abilities, aptitudes, skills and knowledge required for the application should be well defined and based on a sound knowledge of the job under discussion. Test data will

not provide you with good information if you do not know the standards you are seeking.

You also need to set criteria relating to the results. Are you comparing competitively with other job holders/subjects? Are you comparing with the norms? Are you comparing with some pre-set standard?

2 **Use batteries of tests.** In most real situations, a single test may not give wide or comprehensive data across all of the target abilities. Thus, you may need to use a number of tests that provide this range of data. Alternatively, you can use one of the batteries mentioned above or in the digest below to get the required coverage.

3 **Evaluate the proposed tests.** Look at the test supplier's data on reliability and validity. Check if the test/battery is levelled appropriately for your target audience. You might also want to gain some third-party or objective opinion, such as the excellent BPS reviews we will discuss on Thursday. Alternatively, check with your trade association, or, better still, find someone who has used the tests in practice.

4 **Get expert help.** You might use consultants at any or all points in the process:
  ● to advise on test choice
  ● to be a licensed purchaser
  ● to add objectivity to the process
  ● to administer and interpret professionally.

5 **Use results in conjunction with other data.** This is a general rule which makes a lot of sense. We shall talk in more detail about these other kinds of data in the following days.

The list of test suppliers at the back of this book (see Useful contacts) or your professional association are good starting points for tracking down relevant and useful tests.

Summary

Today we have looked at the whole field of ability and aptitude testing. We now know that any ability people have, and any aspect of their behaviour, can be tested for – at least in theory!

You should have some appreciation of the different types of ability tests that are available, what they can measure, and how they differ from personality tests. We have seen that collections or batteries of tests can incorporate verbal, numerical and abstract components, and come in different versions to suit, for example, either general or graduate populations. A key point worth repeating here is that tests should always be set at the level appropriate for the candidates.

This chapter has also given you an insight into how much research was involved in developing some of the best-known ability tests, and how they can be applied to evaluate decision-making skills as well as knowledge. And don't forget the practical tips we gave you in the final section to help you choose a test that will be relevant to your organization's precise needs.

Tomorrow we move on to examine the complex nature of human personality and will learn about the psychometric tests that have been developed in this field.

SUNDAY

MONDAY

TUESDAY

WEDNESDAY

THURSDAY

FRIDAY

SATURDAY

Fact-check (answers at the back)

1. What concept lies at the heart of the development of psychometric testing?
   a) Intellectualism ❏
   b) Individualism ❏
   c) Intelligence ❏
   d) Intuition ❏

2. How do ability tests differ from personality tests?
   a) They are not self-assessed ❏
   b) They involve right–wrong answers ❏
   c) They are administered in rigorous circumstances ❏
   d) They are often timed ❏

3. Which of these is *not* a class of ability test?
   a) Objective ability test ❏
   b) Subjective ability test ❏
   c) Achievement test ❏
   d) Performance test ❏

4. What three kinds of items typically make up general ability tests?
   a) Verbal ❏
   b) Numerical ❏
   c) Alphabetical ❏
   d) Abstract ❏

5. What is the term for a collection of tests?
   a) Set ❏
   b) Sequence ❏
   c) Battery ❏
   d) Array ❏

6. What kind of test is designed to assess a person's ability to assess relationships between shapes and figures?
   a) Academic ❏
   b) Intangible ❏
   c) Abstract ❏
   d) Conceptual ❏

7. Tests should be sensitized to the level of whom?
   a) The examiners ❏
   b) The takers ❏
   c) The administrators ❏
   d) The markers ❏

8. Which of these are critical reasoning abilities?
   a) Deduction ❏
   b) Interpretation ❏
   c) Procrastination ❏
   d) The evaluation of arguments ❏

9. What body developed the Management Self Assessment Test (MSAT)?
   a) Confederation of British Industry ❏
   b) British Psychological Society ❏
   c) Chartered Institute of Personnel and Development ❏
   d) Chartered Management Institute ❏

10. How many questions make up the MSAT?
    a) 7 ❏
    b) 17 ❏
    c) 70 ❏
    d) 170 ❏

WEDNESDAY

What is personality?

We're nearly halfway through the week so let's take stock for a moment. In the past three days, you have examined the purpose of psychometric tests and the way they are designed and validated, as well as reviewed some of the main types. Today we are going to examine one of the most important and perhaps controversial uses of these tests: to gain an insight into the personalities of the people who take them.

To begin with, we shall spend some time studying the nature of personality and the development of modern theories on personality. We will cover personality traits and techniques such as 'factor analysis' and Jungian typology.

Then we will review some of the different applications available to managers, focusing on the key personality tests in use today, including ones you may have already heard of – for example, the Myers-Briggs Type Inventory. The final sections of this chapter will look at two critical issues: the dangers of misinterpreting test results and whether your personality profile can change over time.

By the time you have finished today's work, you should have a clear idea of what personality tests can or cannot do, and be ready to consider the various applications for psychometric tests in organizations, which is Friday's task.

What do we mean by personality?

Ask 20 psychologists to define personality and you will certainly get 20 different answers. What they generally mention, however, is an individual's characteristic patterns of thinking, feeling and acting across a wide range of situations. What are the consistent features of the way they behave? What makes them unique? Already here we have the concepts of consistency and repetition, implying that aspects of personality can be measured.

The development of modern personality theory

Interest in measuring an individual's psychology can be traced back to the Second World War when the need to recruit large numbers of men into the armed forces led to the development of mental aptitude tests in the USA and Britain. Personality testing really did not get off the ground until after the war, although the theory behind these tests was developed by Allport in the 1930s.

Research into the nature of personality has mainly focused on 'personality traits' and on 'typologies'.

Personality traits

Modern theories of personality can still be traced back to the early work of the British anthropologist Francis Galton from 1869 onwards. Galton was interested in the nature of genius, and began his work by reviewing all the words we use to describe personality (the lexicon approach). He then attempted to group these descriptions into a classification scheme. The US psychologist Gordon Allport continued this work in the 1930s, but it was only after the Second World War that the scientific measurement of personality really came into being with the work of another American psychologist, James Cattell.

Cattell began by asking individuals to rate each other using the descriptions of personality used in everyday language. His review of the data suggested that there were no more than about 50 underlying dimensions. Further work with larger samples and the advanced statistical techniques pioneered by Charles Spearman led to his conclusions that there were no more than 12 Life (L) factors involved. Cattell then began to devise questionnaire items to measure these 12 factors and subsequently identified a further four factors (Q) from an analysis of the questionnaire returns.

The 16 primary factors identified by Cattell and now contained in the 16PF test are as follows:

A Warmth	**L** Vigilance
B Reasoning	**M** Abstractness
C Emotional stability	**N** Privateness
E Dominance	**O** Apprehension
F Liveliness	**Q1** Openness to change
G Rule-consciousness	**Q2** Self-reliance
H Social boldness	**Q3** Perfectionism
I Sensitivity	**Q4** Tension

Each factor is measured on a spectrum expressed as word pairs – e.g. Warmth is measured on a scale of *Reserved–Warm*.

Factor analysis

One of the key tools in this research was 'factor analysis', which at its time was a revolutionary technique. Now it is a standard tool used by psychology students all over the world. Fortunately, we do not need to worry about the mathematics involved!

In simple terms, factor analysis studies the correlations between the variables in complex data sets containing many variables (multivariate analysis) and patterns of variation (variance) in the data. Computer programs attempt to distinguish between independent variation in each variable and the variation that can be explained by common unidentified factors linking the different variables. The final output is a list of equations for a series of common factors linked to a figure for the amount of variation in the data set that can be explained by the existence of each factor. Psychologists can then study the nature of these patterns and formulate models for the factors explaining human behaviour.

Cattell used factor analysis to identify the primary factors in his questionnaire.

How personality tests are designed

A personality test is simply a series of questions that assess an individual's thinking, feeling and acting in different situations. Typically these questions will ask you how much you agree or disagree with a statement on a five-point scale, e.g.:

I think personality tests are a load of nonsense.				
strongly agree	agree	not sure	disagree	strongly disagree
O	O	O	O	O

or they ask the test-taker to choose between options, e.g.:

When relaxing, I would prefer to:

(a) listen to some classical music
(b) go and play a game of squash
(select option a or b)

A key feature of these tests is that they measure your stated preferences (often referred to as 'self reports') and are not trying to uncover some hidden part of your nature you would rather cover over. In this respect, they are quite different from the use of handwriting tests, where a single interpreter seeks to identify 'hidden' aspects of your personality from a sample of handwriting.

Jungian typology

The theory of psychological types was developed by the Swiss psychologist Carl Jung (1875–1961) to explain some of the apparently random differences in people's behaviour. Following extensive work on clients and others, Jung discovered predictable and differing patterns of behaviour. His theory of personality types recognized the existence of distinct patterns and provided an explanation for how these types develop.

According to Jung, differences in behaviour are caused by differences in the way people like to use their minds. The central idea is that when your mind is active, you are involved in one of two key mental activities:

1 taking information in, i.e. *Perceiving*, or
2 organizing that information internally and coming to conclusions, i.e. *Judging*.

In turn, Jung observed that there were two opposite ways of Perceiving, which he called *Sensing* and *Intuition*, and two opposite ways of Judging, which he called *Thinking* and *Feeling*. Everyone uses these essential processes on a daily basis, both towards the external world of people, things and events (*Extraversion*) and towards the inner world of ideas, thought and reflection (*Introversion*). These four basic processes provide you with eight different ways of using your mind.

Jung believed that everyone has a natural preference for using one kind of Perceiving and one kind of Judging, and he observed that each was drawn towards either the external or internal world. This idea was later expanded by Katherine Cook Briggs and her daughter, Isabel Briggs Myers, and used to develop the Myers-Briggs Type Indicator (MBTI) instrument.

Today the MBTI is one of the most widely used personality tests, and has been translated into a number of languages. It can provide considerable insight into the way an individual relates to others, and into their preferred team role and work environment.

The MBTI is based on Jung's typology, and reports your preference on four scales, each consisting of two opposite poles:

1 **Extraversion or Introversion (E–I):** where you prefer to focus your attention
2 **Sensing or Intuition (S–N):** the way you prefer to take in information
3 **Thinking or Feeling (T–F):** the way you prefer to make decisions
4 **Judging or Perceiving (J–P):** the way you orientate yourself to the outside world.

Combinations of these four scales give us 16 different types as shown below. Each type can be referred to by a four-letter code.

	ST: Sensing-Thinking	SF: Sensing-Feeling
IJ–Introvert-Judging	ISTJ	ISFJ
IP–Introvert-Perceiving	ISTP	ISFP
EP–Extravert-Perceiving	ESTP	ESFP
EJ–Extravert-Judging	ESTJ	ESFJ
	NF: Intuitive-Feeling	NT: Intuitive-Thinking
IJ–Introvert-Judging	INFJ	INTJ
IP–Introvert-Perceiving	INFP	INTP
EP–Extravert-Perceiving	ENFP	ENTP
EJ–Extravert-Judging	ENFJ	ENTJ

The ESTJ type

Many managers fall into the ESTJ type. Here is an abbreviated description of this type:

'Practical, realistic and matter-of-fact with a natural ability for practical subjects like business or mechanics. They are not interested in abstract theories and expect their learning to have immediate and practical application. They love to organize and run activities. They are decisive, acting quickly to implement decisions and can be relied upon to pay attention to practical, routine issues.'

This seems to be a pretty good description of a typical manager. Of course, this does not mean that the other types make poor managers, and a quick review of the others will highlight those types who make great leaders (e.g. ENTJ) or entrepreneurs (e.g. INTJ).

Typologies have one great advantage: they are easy to understand and to relate to. They are often a great tool for developing individuals and for increasing their awareness of some of their main patterns of behaviour and how others see them. This approach also stresses a key principle about the use of personality scales, namely that there is no right or wrong preference. On the other hand, typologies are generally less suited to selection because they are too simplistic and do not allow us to discriminate clearly between individuals.

The 'Big Five'

Sooner or later, if you talk to anyone about personality tests, you will hear them mention 'the Big Five'. These arose from the work of Costa and McCrae in 1985 who studied the results of a range of personality questionnaires using factor analysis and who identified five big factors that could explain most of the personality space covered by all these different measures. On the basis of this research, they designed the NEO-Personality Inventory (NEO-PI) which measures differences between individuals on the five dimensions described below:

1 **Neuroticism:** high scorers here are generally more sensitive, emotional and prone to feelings that are upsetting such as guilt or sadness. Low scorers are emotionally secure, resistant and relaxed individuals even under very stressful conditions.

2 **Extraversion:** high scorers here are extraverted, outgoing, active and high-spirited. They prefer to be around people most of the time. Low scorers are introverted, reserved and serious. They prefer to be alone or with a few close friends.

3 **Openness to experience:** high scorers here are open to new experiences, with broad interests and a strong imagination. Low scorers are down-to-earth, practical, traditional and pretty much set in their ways.

4 **Agreeableness:** high scorers here are compassionate, good-natured and generally eager to co-operate and avoid conflict. Low scorers are hard-headed, sceptical, proud and competitive. They tend to express their anger directly and forcefully.

5 **Conscientiousness:** high scorers here are conscientious and well organized. They have high standards and always strive to achieve their goals. Low scorers are easy-going, not very well organized and sometimes rather careless. They prefer not to make plans if they can help it.

In fact, these five factors can be related to the global factors found in multifactor tests like the 16PFV5 and 15FQ. They also link to the dimensions in the Jungian typology.

Sometimes the computer printouts from personality tests provide values for dimensions contained in other tests such as the Belbin Roles, Leadership and Subordinate Styles, and Jungian types. These are estimates provided by the test designers and should be treated with caution.

Since the publication of Costa and McCrae's work, the issue of the Big Five has attracted a lot of controversy, mainly on the grounds that they cannot cover all aspects of personality. However, a number of studies across a wide range of occupational groups have in fact shown correlations between ratings on these dimensions and job performance criteria.

Some key personality tests

16PF: the original 16-factor test developed by Cattell that has spawned many similar 15–17 factor tests.

15FQ: a similar instrument to the 16PF produced by Psytech International.

Belbin Team Roles: popular due to availability of the questionnaire in the public domain, the Belbin test has its fans and critics. It does allow companies to combine personal development, team-building activities and job analysis within one activity.

Myers-Briggs Type Indicator (MBTI): already discussed.

NEO-PI: easy to administer and score, this questionnaire evaluates you against the Big Five factors.

OPQ: the Occupational Personality Questionnaire is one of the best-known instruments, and is offered by the SHL Group.

Following Daniel Goleman's (1995) best-seller on emotional intelligence, there has been a surge in the use of tests that attempt to measure individuals against the main factors involved. There are a number of tests available, including the Emotional Competence Inventory (ECI), the Multifactor Emotional Intelligence Scale (MEIS) and the Bar-On Emotional Quotient Inventory (EQ-i).

Other well-known instruments include the California Personality Inventory (CPI), the Gordon Personal Profile Inventory, the Guilford-Zimmerman Temperament Survey and OPP.

Details of some of the main suppliers are provided at the end of this book.

The complex nature of personality

Personality and personal-values questionnaires are relatively cheap and easy to administer and score, but are certainly less reliable and valid than tests of mental ability. Little or no evidence of criterion validity (i.e. relevance to the job) has been found for many personality tests and scales. The fact that the questions themselves often have no relevance to the workplace does not help. In some well-documented cases, their value in selecting people from unusual backgrounds or different cultures has been questioned because test design is heavily influenced by culture.

This does not mean, however, that personality tests do not have an important role to play in organizations. But they must be used intelligently, and users need to recognize their limitations. Even a perfect test (if it existed!) can be misused, and most of the examples used to criticize the use of personality tests are due to misuse of the test and not to the test design itself. Administering the test is the easy part, but the minute a test-user receives the results they enter a danger zone with many traps for the unwary. This is because the two most important stages of test use – interpretation and using the results to make decisions – are profoundly influenced by the situation and may also be left in the hands of those with insufficient expertise.

Misinterpretation of tests

Personality tests are very open to misinterpretation. Your stated preference is just that: it does not mean you always behave that way, and it does need to be placed in the context of your experience, acquired skills and environment. For example, if you are a strong introvert, this does not mean that you are automatically shy, retiring and unable to perform well in social situations. In reality, we all acquire skills that enable us to perform well in areas that may not be our natural preference. We know many consultants who are seen as extreme extraverts but who are actually the opposite, but their lifestyle and job has taught them to behave as extraverts.

Inappropriate use of personality tests also leads people to arrive at the wrong conclusions and to take bad decisions. In selection, for example, you can only use the results of tests successfully if you have shown key features of personality to be critical to the job and have correctly interpreted the results for individuals. Ultimately, the test-taker is probably the best judge of the accuracy of the report, which is why detailed feedback is usually advised.

Does your personality profile change?

Generally, the profiles of most individuals remain stable at least over several years. However, they can be affected by periods of change or stress, and this does need to be taken into account. Over longer periods of time there is no doubt that individuals may 'drift' on individual scales, usually because they have learned new skills and ways of thinking.

People working in highly disciplined professions such as the law or science may develop profiles matching the job requirements more closely. There seems to be some evidence that some effective managers can develop more balanced profiles as they increase their repertoire of behavioural skills (notably in Introversion–Extraversion).

Summary

Today we have covered the basic principles upon which personality tests are designed, including a short discussion of the fundamental nature of personality and how it can be assessed and evaluated. We have looked at personality traits and factor analysis, and learned that personality tests in general are focused on identifying individual preferences on a limited number of dimensions.

If how tests work still sounds complicated, relax! A thorough grasp of the theory and the mathematics is only necessary for psychologists and publishers. The important things for you to understand are the advantages and disadvantages of the various techniques. For instance, typologies are good for the personal development of your existing employees, not so good for the recruitment of new ones.

Furthermore, we have found that special care must be used in the interpretation of test results, and that this, rather than any flaw in the design of a test, is usually the source of inaccurate and/or invalid data. And even if the results are accurate, they will be of no use if the test itself was not relevant to your exact requirements.

Tomorrow we shall turn our attention to some of the practical issues surrounding the selection and application of psychometric tests in organizations.

SUNDAY

MONDAY

TUESDAY

WEDNESDAY

THURSDAY

FRIDAY

SATURDAY

Fact-check (answers at the back)

1. How many primary factors were identified by Cattell?
   a) 10 ❏
   b) 12 ❏
   c) 14 ❏
   d) 16 ❏

2. Which of these is not one of Cattell's primary factors?
   a) Liveliness ❏
   b) Dominance ❏
   c) Submissiveness ❏
   d) Perfectionism ❏

3. What tool did Cattell use to identify the primary factors in his questionnaire?
   a) Figurative analysis ❏
   b) Facial analysis ❏
   c) Factor analysis ❏
   d) Follicle analysis ❏

4. Personality tests measure your stated preferences, which are also referred to as...
   a) First choices ❏
   b) Self-indulgences ❏
   c) Self reports ❏
   d) Favourites ❏

5. Who developed the theory of psychological types?
   a) Karl Marx ❏
   b) Carl Jung ❏
   c) Sigmund Freud ❏
   d) Edward de Bono ❏

6. Tests like the Myers-Briggs Type Inventory can reveal an individual's preferred...
   a) Brand of coffee ❏
   b) Team role ❏
   c) Work environment ❏
   d) Holiday destination ❏

7. Which of these is not one of the 'Big Five' factors identified by Costa and McCrae?
   a) Neuroticism ❏
   b) Rationalism ❏
   c) Agreeableness ❏
   d) Conscientiousness ❏

8. Which of these are key personality tests in use today?
   a) 16PF ❏
   b) 15FQ ❏
   c) B&Q ❏
   d) OPQ ❏

9. What are the two most important stages of the testing process?
   a) Inviting candidates to sit a test ❏
   b) Choosing a location for the test ❏
   c) Interpretation ❏
   d) Using the results to make decisions ❏

10. What factors can cause an individual's personality profile to change?
    a) Periods of stress ❏
    b) Getting a haircut ❏
    c) Learning new skills ❏
    d) Learning new ways of thinking ❏

THURSDAY

Selecting psychometric tests

We will look in more detail today at what is involved in selecting and using tests within a recruitment context.

Getting the selection process right is essential if you are to reap the full benefits of psychometric testing. The first steps are to identify the critical requirements of the job in question and then compile a profile of the perfect candidate. These criteria should then be prioritized as it is highly unlikely that any single applicant will be able to satisfy all of them.

Employers should also remember that the more traditional assessment methods – applications forms, CVs, interviews, references, and so on – still have their place in recruitment. We will explain the pros and cons for each one, which will help you to decide which one(s) your organization should still consider using to balance out data gathered from psychometric testing.

To help you select the right test itself, this chapter also contains some useful pointers on checking the standardization, reliability and validity of tests, including how to make use of professional reviews. In the final section, there is guidance on how to ensure the results of any personality tests conducted by your organization are always interpreted correctly.

The selection process

Even if we know a psychometric test is reliable and valid, we can only exploit its full potential with an effective selection process. Most people can recall examples where candidates for a job have been exposed to a pretty gruelling procedure only to have all that effort wasted by one interviewer's prejudices. Before we can use a test, therefore, we must consider all aspects of the selection process.

Identifying job requirements

In most selection situations, it is useful to regard the selection process as a process that brings together all the information we gain about an applicant, in the form of an 'applicant profile'. This profile will not just contain information about their personality but will also include information on their abilities and aptitudes, their qualifications and training, and their experience, as well as any other general information relevant to the job in question. This applicant profile clearly relates to the concept of an ideal job profile or 'person specification', which typically consists of a list of criteria matching our idealized impression of the job holder. Of course, this ideal rarely matches reality, so we are forced to discriminate between the essential and the desirable, and then to compare individual applicant profiles against this final profile.

If we are supplied with a good job spec, the task of producing the ideal applicant profile should be relatively easy. However, it is always worth reviewing the job spec in a wider context to ensure that it is based on reality, not just on optimistic goals, and is expressed in terms of the specific tasks required for the post. From these, we should be able to clearly identify the critical qualities for fulfilling the requirements of the job.

This is the theory at least, but typically job specs are produced by line managers and may not be that accurate. It is important to recognize that effective recruitment and selection of the workforce should form just one part of an integrated strategy for improving the quality of the workforce with several key components, as shown in the figure below.

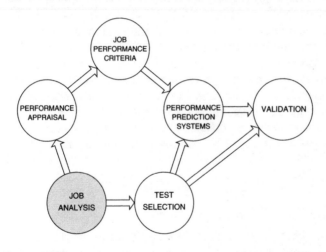

- **Job analysis** is the starting point, and can be achieved using several different techniques. Job-analysis interviews and questionnaires can identify the elements that are most relevant to different jobs. A more specialized approach is the use of Repertory Grid Analysis (RGA) or Critical Incident Analysis (CIA) to clarify the characteristics of successful job holders.
- **Performance appraisal systems** should of course reflect the key elements of a job identified by detailed job analysis. Staff need to be trained to implement the system in a consistent and reliable manner.

- **Job performance criteria** need to be identified that will allow the organization to link assessment criteria (and therefore chosen tests) to job performance.
- **Performance prediction systems** will ultimately enable us to fine-tune human-resource planning and assessment techniques.
- **Validation** is of course the key to the system, and should seek to determine whether individuals selected under the new system really do perform better than through previous procedures. One approach is to compare the performance of samples of employees selected under different systems.

Prioritizing requirements

No recruitment and selection process can cover all aspects of human behaviour, nor is any one individual likely to fulfil all requirements. The importance of prioritizing these requirements cannot be overemphasized. It is common for organizations to use a weighting scheme in the selection process (i.e. different dimensions are given different levels of importance), and, although this may seem somewhat bureaucratic, the discussion of both the weightings and the results among the decision-makers is really what matters.

Reviewing the assessment methods available

Psychometric tests are just one method of assessing individuals. Their great advantage is their ease of use and low cost, but they do require access to the right sort of expertise and may have relatively low job relevance. Organizations should carry out a comprehensive review of all the methods available to them.

Here, with their advantages and disadvantages, are some of the options that should be considered when looking to balance psychometric data with other types of data:

- **Application form:** this is a method of collecting information at the early stages of the selection process. It is standardized in structure, but provides minimal data.

- **Curriculum vitae:** this is a method of evaluating career history and achievements. It can build up a good picture of a candidate, but it is not standardized and needs verifying.
- **References and testimonials:** this is third-party data about an individual. At best, it can give a picture of a person's strengths through the eyes of a stakeholder. However, it is not standardized, and it is likely to be subjective.
- **Biodata:** this is biographical data based on forced choice questions. It can be very effective when standardized, objective and verified. However, it has to be custom designed and evaluated.
- **Biographical interview:** this is a structured interview covering education, achievements, interests, career and relationships. A more recent development is the competence-based interview which focuses on individual style and achievement in relation to a specific competence framework. The biographical interview produces high-quality data if structured appropriately. However, it needs a great deal of skill to construct and to conduct. It also needs an appropriate competence framework to underwrite it.
- **Records of qualification and achievement:** these are what as the name implies. They are objective and easily obtainable, but they are limited in scope.
- **Performance appraisal:** this comprises information about performance in the job; such appraisal adds some objective data from a range of stakeholders. A performance appraisal provides good data if conducted reliably, and the 360-degree process can be particularly powerful. However, it is difficult to obtain or verify as a third party. It is also time consuming.
- **Assessment centre:** this involves candidates in a variety of activities and exercises, each of which is designed to provide data on different aspects of aptitude, skill and knowledge in terms of real behaviour in realistic situations. It produces a range of very powerful data on behaviour in realistic situations. However, it is also expensive and time consuming.
- **Interview:** already discussed, this provides first-hand data and impressions of the person involved. However, and again as mentioned above, it is not very accurate, objective and reliable.

Selecting the right tests

Every manager considering the optimum mix of tests to use within current constraints of time and resources is faced with a dilemma:

- Should they select or even design a specific test that gives a precise and highly reliable measurement of a limited but critical aspect of a job, *or*
- Should they use a variety of tests that are less precise and predictive, but which provide a broader and more comprehensive range of competencies?

Given the pace of change in the modern work environment, there is probably a tendency to use broader-based tools.

In the final analysis, test-users should be committed to using only those tests which can be shown to meet the

CLOSING THE
SALE
APPRAISAL
TEST

purpose for which they are to be used and that are appropriate for the intended test-takers. This means test-users should:

- define the purpose of the testing, and identify the target population
- select a test that matches the purpose and population, based on a thorough review of all available information, including, where possible, independent test reviews
- read all the support materials provided by test developers, and avoid using tests where the information in these materials is unclear or incomplete
- ensure they become familiar with the background to the test's development, and that they understand the technical research data underpinning the test
- examine specimen materials, including questionnaires, test instructions, answer sheets, manuals, scored results and computer feedback reports, before selecting a test.

This is clearly a rather rigorous process and a little off-putting. Small wonder that some organizations are inclined to cut corners and leave the decision to an expert. If you are tempted to do this, remind yourself that careless selection of tests has landed some large organizations in an industrial tribunal. At the very least, your selection process will be flawed and you can expect poorer results.

Checklist for selecting a test

Let's imagine that you have followed the process through and are about to make a final decision on the use of one or more tests. Before you fix on your choice, it will probably be useful to double-check your findings against the following checklist:

- Do you have enough evidence that the test measures a key requirement for the job concerned? Has a proper job analysis or validation study been carried out?
- Does the test come with a manual that provides technical information and instructions for test administration?
- Is there an alternative form of the test in case you need to administer it a second time or one of them is compromised?
- Is there an objective scoring key?
- Is each of the scales measured statistically reliable?
- Is there evidence of validity for the type of job and population targeted?
- Are there published norms for the targeted job and population?
- Do you have someone trained to administer, score and interpret the scores?

Checking the standardization, reliability and validity of tests

On Monday you learned about the importance of norms, reliability and validity. These issues are especially relevant to the use of personality tests for two reasons:

1 **Personality tests are normative,** i.e. individual results are always scored by comparing them to the rest of the population. Quoting a score without referencing it to the general population or to some specific sector such as professionals or managers is meaningless.
2 **Personality tests are not infallible.** Unless we have some measure of their accuracy and their relevance to the issues we wish to explore, then once again we will be on shaky

ground and in danger of misinterpreting the results. Even as a test-user, we need to check out the three issues of norms, reliability and validity.

Norms

Employers using personality tests must be confident that the test is not subject to bias, or, where there is bias (e.g. sex differences), that any discrimination that does arise is real and justified in terms of the job itself.

Here are some guidelines on what you are looking for:

- **Size of sample:** this should be at least 1,000, evenly distributed between males and females.
- **Norm populations:** the overall sample for the general population should be taken from a wide range of organizations. Check the range of organizations used: a sample of three companies probably does not represent a balanced sample.
- **Specialized norm groups:** norm tables for groups closely related to your intended target should be provided.

Reliability

Most modern tests are very reliable in terms of the design of items, given the free availability of computer software for item analysis. However, you do need to pay attention to test–retest reliability, which is a measure of the accuracy of the test. Obviously, it is not sensible to use a test whose results can vary considerably.

Validity

The fact that a test has high reliability, i.e. that it produces consistent results, is no guarantee that it is actually measuring what the publisher claims it does (construct validity) or, more importantly, that it will provide useful information to the decision-maker (criterion-based validity). Ask yourself whether what you are seeing really matches what you are seeking in your organization.

Using professional reviews

There are a number of sources of help in obtaining high-quality evaluative information about tests, and a number of these have been mentioned throughout the week. One excellent source is the British Psychological Society which publishes reviews of ability and aptitude tests, as well as of personality assessment instruments. These reviews consist of independent and rigorous test evaluations in common use. Each review consists of:

- test details
- general information
- administration and scoring
- documentation
- evaluation.

They are a good source of both information and reassurance.

The interpretation of test results

There is a common perception that companies use personality tests to discover our weaknesses. Among cynics, the regulation of the use of tests is seen as a way of increasing their mystique and of sewing up the market. While it cannot be denied that certain publishers use some restrictions for commercial

INTERESTING ... AN UNCONTROLLABLE WEAKNESS FOR HAM SANDWICHES

benefit, the truth is that the restricted use of tests and the professional code of practice applied in the UK are ultimately for the protection of the user.

When interpreting results, we often find people suffer from misconceptions as to what the tests show. Here are some simple principles that are often ignored:

- There is no such thing as a right or wrong personal profile. Scoring high or low on one dimension is a measure not of how good you are but of how unusual you are!
- Extreme personalities are interesting to us, but so are typical or average scores on personality dimensions. Someone who shows an average level of assertiveness will generally seek to gain a balance between being preoccupied with getting the job done to achieve results (whatever the cost!) and adapting to changed circumstances, quickly finding new solutions.
- We can only talk about the degree of match between your profile and the job or circumstances you find yourself in.

- When there is a mismatch, people can experience discomfort or learn to adapt. An individual's natural preference is not the same as their observed behaviour.
- The words used to describe personality traits are often emotive in common language and need professional interpretation. For that reason, computer reports tend to read like astrology forecasts ('You may be inclined to...' 'It is possible you may feel anger...').
- Everything is relative, including our own reaction to the results. The use of the label 'sensitive' or 'sentimental' simply means you will probably appreciate music, the arts, a film or book with a creative or emotive theme more than a practical hobby, an action-packed film, a detective novel or a biography.

Summary

The main points to remember from today's discussion involve not just the tests themselves and the wider selection process but also three other vital elements.

The first of these is selecting the test or battery of tests appropriate to your organization's requirements. We have taken you through the basic points you need to consider when choosing a test – from identifying the target population to examining specimen materials. We then provided you with a detailed checklist to help you choose a test that is unbiased, reliable and valid.

Second, we stressed the importance of defining and following a process to deliver the required results. Look back at the four golden rules for using personality tests, the first of which was that test results should be interpreted by a suitable expert. This leads on to the third key point – namely, that the selection process and the data it produces should be reviewed and evaluated at every stage.

Selecting the wrong test, or administering the right test incorrectly, can be costly: you could end up with data that is practically useless, leading you to appoint someone to a position which is beyond their ability, or, in the worst-case scenario, even find yourself facing legal action for unfair discrimination from a disgruntled candidate.

SUNDAY

MONDAY

TUESDAY

WEDNESDAY

THURSDAY

FRIDAY

SATURDAY

Fact-check (answers at the back)

1. Even if a psychometric test is reliable and valid, its full potential can only be exploited with an effective...
   - a) Office computer ❏
   - b) Office printer ❏
   - c) Office tea rota ❏
   - d) Selection process ❏

2. In order to produce the ideal applicant profile, it is essential to have an accurate...
   - a) Photograph ❏
   - b) Job specification ❏
   - c) Watch ❏
   - d) Horoscope ❏

3. What do organizations commonly use to prioritize requirements during the selection process?
   - a) Quotas ❏
   - b) A weight loss plan ❏
   - c) A weighting scheme ❏
   - d) A waiting room ❏

4. What is the missing word in this sentence: 'The attention paid to the assessment of individual dimensions should be in direct proportion to the _____ of the dimension'?
   - a) Size ❏
   - b) Extent ❏
   - c) Length ❏
   - d) Importance ❏

5. When selecting a test, one of the first things you should do is identify the target...
   - a) Price ❏
   - b) Customer ❏
   - c) Population ❏
   - d) Market ❏

6. What kind of specimen materials should you look at before selecting a test?
   - a) Questionnaires ❏
   - b) Instructions ❏
   - c) Answer sheets ❏
   - d) Manuals ❏

7. As individual results are always scored by comparing them to the rest of the population, personality tests are classified as...
   - a) Normal ❏
   - b) Abnormal ❏
   - c) Normative ❏
   - d) Informative ❏

8. When comparing scores to the rest of the population, how big should be the size of the sample?
   - a) At least 100 ❏
   - b) At least 1,000 ❏
   - c) At least 10,000 ❏
   - d) At least 100,000 ❏

9. What areas would a rigorous independent review of a test cover?
   - a) Administration ❏
   - b) Scoring ❏
   - c) Documentation ❏
   - d) Evaluation ❏

10. Which of these are recognized sources of supporting evidence that you can use to confirm the results of a personality test?
    - a) Testimonials ❏
    - b) Peer reviews ❏
    - c) Facebook ❏
    - d) Assessment centres ❏

FRIDAY

The uses of psychometric tests

If you've got that Friday feeling, you will be pleased to hear that today's discussion is not too taxing. It will be a review of the wider range of uses for psychometric tests within organizations.

The most popular uses for testing are screening, shortlisting and placement during the recruitment process. Other applications in the modern workplace could be to support change management and employee engagement, quality initiatives and retraining programmes.

We will also examine the growing trend to use tests for personal development and as an aid to career counselling. We explain the conditions that need to be met in order for tests used in this context to be effective, and consider a case study from the Chartered Management Institute.

Personality tests can yield significant information about how an individual interacts with other people, and what role they are best suited for in a team environment. We introduce you to two such tests: the Belbin Team Role Inventory and the Learning Styles Inventory, both self-scored tests that are widely used to help construct more efficient teams.

We finish the chapter with a brief look at tests that can reveal an individual's values and interests, and what this can tell us about their career.

The range of uses for tests

Psychological tests can serve a variety of uses in an organization. In the coming pages, we shall consider some of the more important ones.

Screening and shortlisting

By selecting this option, the management team is also deciding that for the job in question it would prefer to employ people with more developed skills in a particular area. The managers concerned need to be committed to the importance of the abilities in question, and candidates, on their part, will expect to be given a fair opportunity to demonstrate their potential.

In combination with other methods of assessment

Tests are probably best viewed as an integral part of the complete assessment of an individual, rather like examining the pieces that make up a complete jigsaw. They might be used, for example, to identify some key issues that can be explored in greater depth in a subsequent interview. Alternatively, they may provide complementary evidence, confirming aspects of behaviour or competencies identified by other means (e.g. 360-degree surveys, assessment centres – see Thursday).

The challenge for anyone interpreting results is to tease out the possible explanations for any inconsistencies in

performance and to arrive at a reasoned and valid judgement about a candidate's true ability or personal disposition. Weighing up and evaluating psychometric results effectively requires experience and judgement, but in the right hands it leads to a more rounded and balanced evaluation of an individual's true strengths and weaknesses.

Placement

A detailed study of individuals using personality tests and questionnaires can play a valuable role in matching individuals to jobs that best suit them, thereby helping management to make optimum use of the human resources available to them.

Other applications

Creative managers can in fact identify many uses for psychometric tests in the workplace.

- A newly appointed chief executive could use tests to handle sensitive issues relating to the senior manager group in a takeover or merger. Not only can they provide an insight into the nature of the team, especially if performance records/ feedback are limited or missing, but they can also provide a source of information to support future decisions on deployment, promotion, development and outplacements.
- Tests can support initiatives to improve the quality of work performance in change or quality initiatives.
- In a company with sensitive industrial relations, the use of tests to identify the potential for retraining and job changes can significantly reduce the potential for conflict in the workplace.

Personal development

One of the most exciting trends has been the growing use of tests to enrich an individual's insight into their own capability, potential and development needs. Providing individuals with professional feedback on test results in a career counselling session allows them to gain a better understanding of their personal qualities and to take ownership of their own development process.

Using psychometrics for development: a case study

The UK's Chartered Management Institute has had great success with numerous organizations using a combination of tools for assessment. The chosen tools are:

1 **MSAT.** This applied judgement test has already been described (see Tuesday), and it provides objective data on the knowledge, judgement and critical thinking of subjects in the context of realistic management situations.

2 **a psychometric test.** This is usually a factor-based test such as 16PFi or the similar 15FQ+. It often provides the 'backdrop' or the underlying rationale or explanation for why people behave the way they do at work.

3 **a 360-degree assessment process.** This is a quantitative assessment based on a competence framework (either the organization's own or one based on the Institute's own competence data bank). It involves polling up to 15 stakeholders, and provides a comprehensive quantitative picture of the behaviour of the subject as seen through the eyes of others.

The above is a comprehensive and thoroughgoing approach which is somewhat unusual in its scope and depth. However, for the individuals involved, the 'three-dimensional' data it provides is often the most powerful that they have ever received.

Because of the quantitative nature of the data, it is possible to aggregate it. This enables the data to be analysed using some sophisticated statistical techniques (e.g. factor analysis and cluster analysis). This in turn generates a very comprehensive picture at corporate level that encompasses competence, roles, culture and so on.

For the use of personality tests to be effective, a number of conditions need to apply:

● Subjects need to be volunteers not conscripts
● The test instrument must have a good level of face validity

- Written reports are not as powerful as a feedback discussion with someone qualified and experienced
- Such discussions need to be developmental – i.e. 'What can I do now I know this?'

One of the conclusions that can be drawn from such experience is that, as with selection, psychometric tests work very well in conjunction with other data derived from different sources.

Team construction and team building

Questionnaires like the Myers-Briggs Type Indicator and Belbin's Team Role Inventory can provide considerable insight into the way a person interrelates with others, their preferred role in group situations and their favoured work environment. This can help members of a team to understand each other's strengths and weaknesses and to avoid dangerous blind spots in the way a team functions.

The Belbin Team Role Inventory

The Belbin Team Role Inventory is widespread in its use and recognition. In many organizations, the development that goes with certain levels of seniority is often accompanied by some consideration of the team roles. For this reason, and because of its high face validity, it is worth considering briefly the Inventory itself.

Dr Meredith Belbin, in his research on behaviour with people in group environments, suggested that there are eight primary roles which people adopt in teams:

1 **Shaper:** the drivers of the objectives and priorities, and the agenda setters, these tend to be dominant, dynamic individuals.
2 **Chairman:** this individual controls the way in which the team moves towards the group objectives; he or she makes the team cohere and tends to be dominant and dynamic.
3 **Monitor-Evaluator:** this individual analyses problems and evaluates ideas and suggestions; he or she is analytical, tenacious – a critic.

4 **Plant:** this individual is the ideas generator: creating new approaches; he or she is unorthodox, intelligent, imaginative.

5 **Team Worker:** this individual supports team members, builds the team spirit; he or she is diplomatic and sympathetic.

6 **Company Worker:** this individual translates ideas into action; he or she is a stable, cautious organizer.

7 **Completer-Finisher:** this individual is oriented to the achievement of goals and the completion of tasks; he or she is disciplined and conscientious.

8 **Resource Investigator:** this individual is oriented to communication and contact with the outside world; he or she is extravert, enthusiastic and likeable.

There is a simple self-scored test that will help you to define your own preferred team role and team-role profile. It has proved very useful when members of a team discuss their own preferred team roles and how these operate in terms of the actual team processes.

The Learning Styles Inventory

Another framework, which also has a self-scored test instrument widely available, is the Learning Styles Inventory of D. Honey and A. Mumford. This is based on the learning cycle of David Kolb, an American psychologist. Kolb said that learning is a cyclical process involving a number of components:

- Experience
- Experimenting
- Observation/Reflection
- Theorizing/Conceptualizing.

Honey and Mumford suggested that people have a repertoire of behaviours and preferences in relation to this learning cycle. That is, we have strengths and weaknesses, and are not all equally skilled at each of these stages.

The Learning Styles Inventory is a test instrument that gives a subject a profile of scores against four learning styles, so enabling them to identify their own preferred learning style. The four learning styles are:

1 **The Activist:** this is someone whose preferred style is to engage in new experiences. They enjoy getting involved in here-and-now activities. They enjoy the 'buzz' or risk of new activities.

2 **The Reflector:** reflectors like to take time, and think things through from various angles before acting. They are cautious and measured, and mull over information before reaching conclusions. They don't like to be rushed or pressurized.

3 **The Theorist:** this individual assimilates, integrates and synthesizes information about the world into rational schemes. They are interested in principles, assumptions, objectivity and logic.

4 **The Pragmatist:** this individual values new ideas, not as an end in themselves, but to see if they work in practice. They are down to earth and enjoy getting on with practical activities and problem-solving.

People who are engaged in development processes are often encouraged to test their own profile for Learning Styles. The Inventory has a very high level of face validity and has the benefit of confirming and reassuring people that their natural preferences for learning are sound. Thus, it can help them to make choices about the range of development activities that will suit their style.

It is also known that learning styles can be volatile, or at least sensitive to the changing context of the subject. The good side of this story is that people can change or develop their repertoire of learning approaches along with new experiences.

Other tests

The purpose of this book is not to provide a complete digest of all of the tests, or indeed of all of the test types, that are available. We would need many more than seven days to do that! However, we shall use this section to paint a picture of just some of the many other tests and classes that are available.

There is a class of tests that are used for research, clinical and therapeutic purposes and that have little relevance to organizational life. They are so specialized that we will not consider them here. However, there is another complete class of tests that we have not yet discussed, and these are tests that relate to values and interests. In fact, there are many such tests that give information about what people value and about life interests, going on then to relate this to interests in relation to types of career. An example is the work of John Holland who classified career theme interests into the following categories:

- Realistic
- Investigative
- Artistic
- Social
- Enterprising
- Conventional.

Here are some other aspects of personal and behavioural preference for which there are test instruments:

- selling styles
- management style
- conflict style
- creativity
- motivation
- stress
- leadership.

And there are many more...

Summary

After today you should have more of an appreciation of the versatility of personality tests. We have suggested a whole range of areas within the context of working life where tests might be appropriate, and have looked more specifically at a number of tests that have a very wide usage and currency in organizations.

You should also understand by now that tests are not the be-all and end-all in terms of a recruitment tool. Rather, they should be used alongside other assessment methods, providing additional information that helps to compile a complete picture of an individual.

We have also seen today that psychometric testing has its uses outside the selection process, notably for personal development where again it has been shown that the data produced by testing works well with information from other sources. The combined results give a comprehensive overview of both competencies and preferences, helping individuals to plan their careers.

These insights can also prove invaluable in team building, by identifying people's preferred learning styles and the roles they would like to fulfil in a team environment.

So, just one more day to go. Tomorrow we will look at the issues associated with testing from the perspective of organizations.

SUNDAY
MONDAY
TUESDAY
WEDNESDAY
THURSDAY
FRIDAY
SATURDAY

Fact-check (answers at the back)

1. Besides selection, in what other areas could managerial decisions be supported by the results of psychometric tests?
   a) Deployment ❑
   b) Promotion ❑
   c) Deciding whom to ask to make the tea ❑
   d) Outplacements ❑

2. For personality tests to be effective, which of these conditions need to apply?
   a) Subjects need to be volunteers ❑
   b) A good level of face validity ❑
   c) Feedback discussions ❑
   d) Sunny weather ❑

3. There has been a growing and exciting trend for psychometric tests to be used for what purpose?
   a) Market research ❑
   b) Fitness training ❑
   c) Personal development ❑
   d) Time and motion studies ❑

4. What can questionnaires identify that will contribute to team building?
   a) Strengths of team members ❑
   b) Weaknesses of team members ❑
   c) The team's favourite pub ❑
   d) Preferred roles of team members ❑

5. Which of these is *not* one of the eight primary roles which people adopt in teams as suggested by Belbin?
   a) Chairman ❑
   b) Monitor-Evaluator ❑
   c) Hunter-Gatherer ❑
   d) Completer-Finisher ❑

6. Again, which of these is *not* one of the eight primary roles which people adopt in teams as suggested by Belbin?
   a) Shaper ❑
   b) Fixer ❑
   c) Plant ❑
   d) Company Worker ❑

7. Which of these are components of the learning cycle that underpins the Learning Styles Inventory?
   a) Expectation ❑
   b) Experience ❑
   c) Experimenting ❑
   d) Expression ❑

8. Which of these are styles that can be identified using the Learning Styles Inventory?
   a) The Activist ❑
   b) The Reflector ❑
   c) The Theorist ❑
   d) The Pragmatist ❑

9. Which of these are not among the categories of career themes as classified by Holland?
a) Realistic ☐
b) Idealistic ☐
c) Conventional ☐
d) Unconventional ☐

10. For which of these other aspects of personal and behavioural preference are tests available?
a) Selling style ☐
b) Dress style ☐
c) Management style ☐
d) Conflict style ☐

SATURDAY

The organizational perspective

In our final discussion, we are going to draw the threads together of all the various aspects of psychometric testing that we have covered this week. For the most part, we have considered testing within its own context. What we shall do today is look at it from the point of view of the organization, and examine the implications for those responsible for running tests.

The first section of this chapter will focus on how you can become an accredited user. Organizations can, of course, rely on outside experts to administer and interpret tests but developing in-house expertise can often be a better option. We will give you guidance on how to get qualified, explaining exactly what you will need to know.

Next, we will consider the ethical use of psychometric testing. An obvious point is to ensure you provide candidates with ample information about the testing process. We will also advise you on how to promote equal opportunities. Other areas covered include the secure storage of testing materials and the correct disposal of unwanted records.

Lastly, we look at how organizations can establish their own guidelines for using tests, and what topics you should explore to increase your knowledge and understanding of psychometric testing.

Becoming an accredited user

Once an organization decides to use or develop psychometric tests, it has three options to choose from:

1 using expert advice
2 using a bureau service, *or*
3 developing in-house expertise.

Properly developed tests are only available in the UK to people who are properly trained in their use. If your company has no qualified staff to administer and interpret tests, it must buy in outside expertise. Of course, there are many suppliers of psychometric tests who may support these with public and in-company training courses.

However, using the right expertise for the administration of tests is just the start of the process. It is far more important that your organization give some thought to the best way to select, interpret and develop the applications involving tests. For this you need to build up expertise within the organization and take ownership of processes. Choosing a reputable bureau service may seem a simple decision to take, but in the long term will that option automatically deliver the best decisions for the company?

Getting qualified

Although psychometric tests can significantly improve human-resource decisions, this can be achieved only by the competent use of these instruments. Inappropriate use can not only destroy the effectiveness of a well-thought-out selection process but it can also have a damaging impact on the test-takers themselves. To gain the required level of competence, you need expertise in:

- selecting, administering and scoring tests
- interpreting the results in the specific context of the application for which they are being used
- appreciating the underlying statistics and methodology used to generate the results
- understanding the limitations of tests
- presenting complex information in the best form to decision-makers and test-takers.

For this reason, access to psychometric test materials in the UK and many other countries is restricted to those who are suitably qualified. Organizations need to recognize the importance of this protection and should themselves take steps to ensure that all test applications are handled only by qualified personnel.

Even if you do not want to become qualified yourself, it is still wise to familiarize yourself with some of the key issues in test assessment before making any important decisions on the use of test materials. Without this grounding, you will not be in a position, for example, to critically evaluate the growing number of tests available, along with the claims made by their publishers. Many providers offer short programmes on the basic use of psychometric tests.

Even if you have received some form of general grounding, you may want to consider becoming qualified in the administration and interpretation of tests to the British Psychological Society's standards, i.e:

- **the British Psychological Society's (BPS) Level A Certificate of Competence in Occupational Testing:** Level A covers the general foundations of testing, and the performance skills associated with test administration and interpretation for ability tests.

- **the BPS's Level B Certificate of Competence in Occupational Testing:** Level B complements Level A. It increases the scope of the scheme to include personality assessment. It covers the use and interpretation of personality tests. Level B can be gained only after you have gained a Level A qualification.

If you have gained qualifications outside the UK, you may write to the BPS to have your qualifications recognized as the equivalent of Level A and B. As a user, you can also check whether experts are registered on the BPS register for qualified test personnel.

Finally, many publishers offer conversion training for the use of their own psychometric tests on the grounds that their instruments are sufficiently distinct from others to justify some form of test-specific training. This is a somewhat controversial issue in psychological circles as it is seen by some as a somewhat questionable commercial device to maximize return and impose some form of protectionism. Certainly responsible, qualified experts can be expected to familiarize themselves with all aspects of a test which they are considering using.

The ethical use of tests

Most people tend to view uncertainty and change with unease and distrust, especially if it affects their job opportunities and careers. The user of tests has an important responsibility to recognize and deal with these natural fears, as well as to administer tests properly. The introduction of 'scientific' tests may well be met with negative responses from the workforce. Those who have not studied recently may find them daunting and with no obvious relationship to the day-to-day realities of the workplace. Test-users must take their responsibilities to the test-takers just as seriously as they do those towards the organization.

Communication

Any user of tests must take special steps to provide adequate information to clarify and clear up possible misunderstandings. Without this buy-in, you cannot expect potential test-takers to participate willingly or sit the tests without the potential for unreliable results. The purpose of the tests, the way in which they are developed and applied, and the treatment of data must be explained in such a way as to gain acceptance from the test-takers.

> ### Candidate care
>
> Before embarking on tests, provide the test-taker with adequate information regarding the use of the test, the procedure involved, the likely duration of the test and the likely outcome of the assessment process. Offer guidance and support only in a way that is consistent with the test administration instructions and does not invalidate the process.

Equal opportunities and culture fairness

There are some very simple steps managers can take to promote equal opportunities:

1 **Evaluate the tests.** Check out the procedures used by the test developers to avoid insensitive content or language and to identify potential bias.
2 **Review the performance of test-takers.** Compare the performance of test-takers of different gender and ethnic origin when samples of sufficient size are available.

3 **Modify the test administration if necessary.** Where necessary and feasible, use modified forms or altered administration procedures for test-takers with disabilities. Where bias in tests has been demonstrated, identify the cause with the help of expert advice or consider scrapping the use of the test.

Test administration and scoring

The facilities used for testing are critical. Candidates must be provided with a quiet, well-illuminated and ventilated room, complete with properly spaced tables and chairs. The tests must be carried out under the control of a properly trained administrator and be free from any interruptions, otherwise the test results are invalid.

Test feedback

As a general rule, you should take steps to ensure that test-takers are provided with adequate feedback from a qualified expert. Certainly, where tests are used in selection, you must ensure that all candidates are treated equally. Avoid the temptation to treat internal candidates differently from external applicants because one-to-one feedback is expensive; if in doubt, make sure all test-takers are treated the same.

There will also be situations where it may in fact be ill-advised to provide detailed feedback. Providing too much insight into the assessment methodology might allow individuals to deliberately practise their skills in key areas and so lead to corruption of the process.

Security and access

All test materials should be stored securely, with access restricted to trained test-users. Users should respect the copyright on test materials and inform publishers of any infringements that come to light. Ultimately, this is in the user's interest since any infringement of copyright will probably mean that the test might be corrupted by being passed on to the public.

Locked storage facilities, accompanied by proper company policies governing security and access to personal information, are a must for any test-user. Access must be strictly limited to those who genuinely need to know the test results. Test data must also be used only for the purpose for which it is intended and for which informed consent has been obtained.

Lastly, any automated storage of results means that the individuals concerned have rights of access to the information under the provisions of the Data Protection Act. Since October 1998, this has included non-electronic forms of systematic data collection.

Disposal
Most important, when the purpose for which the tests were used has been achieved, the user must ensure that steps are taken to dispose of any paperwork properly. Unfortunately, test results can all too often be retained far beyond their shelf-life.

Guidelines for using tests in organizations

Even the best test can deliver flawed information when it forms part of a poorly designed process. It is therefore good practice to establish a comprehensive policy on testing and to issue clear guidance to all those involved in the use of tests. Such a policy should identify:

- on what basis tests will be used
- who will take decisions on the use of tests
- who will have access to results
- how the results will be used and incorporated within decision-making processes
- how equal-opportunities issues will be dealt with
- the policy for confidentiality and providing feedback.

Organizations like the Chartered Institute of Personnel and Development, as well as major publishers, can offer a lot of help in this area. Saville & Holdsworth issues a series of *Guidelines for Best Practice* in the selection and recruitment process.

Next steps

This book has equipped you with the basic information that should help you to separate between fact and fiction and to understand more clearly how, as a manager or personnel professional, you can introduce tests into your organization or use them more effectively. However, the use of psychometric tests is a complex subject, and we have only been able to review the main topics superficially.

Getting the best out of tests really requires managers to take ownership of the issue of test use, rather than delegating it to the personnel department. To achieve this, management teams need to become informed about all of the topics covered in this book.

We certainly hope that reading this introduction is just a beginning and that you may wish to cross the threshold into a deeper knowledge and increased ability to apply psychological tests. Some topics you might wish to explore include:

- assessing learning styles in your staff and accommodating these within your frameworks for training and development
- designing company-wide systems to help employees improve personal effectiveness

- using assessment or development centres to exploit and develop staff skills
- identifying the critical factors for success in your most effective employees, and perhaps separating between fact and fantasy.

There are many ways you can increase your knowledge and understanding, such as:

- attending workshops and conferences
- reading books and journal articles on the subject
- joining or forming a discussion group, either by meeting or through the Internet
- discussing topics with your colleagues and friends
- joining a professional association with an interest in this area, so that you are kept informed of events, resources and new developments in the field
- writing to test publishers to gain more information about their instruments and support materials
- gaining qualifications in test administration and interpretation.

Summary

SUNDAY
MONDAY
TUESDAY
WEDNESDAY
THURSDAY
FRIDAY
SATURDAY

Over the last seven days, we have covered a lot of ground on psychometric tests and how to use them. Let's pause one last time to reflect on what we have learned so far...

After this brief introduction – and this book was meant to be no more than that – you should be able to:

● explain how psychometric tests are constructed and how they developed

● recall what aptitudes and abilities can be tested and how

● recognize some well-known and commonly used tests of ability and personality

● evaluate tests for use in selection processes

● understand some of the issues involved in using tests for other processes such as development and team-building

● appreciate some of the issues involved in using tests in an organizational setting

● know where and in what circumstances to seek further information and help.

This week we hope we have dispelled a few myths and, at the same time, spelled out a few home truths. We also hope you feel a little wiser and, if you have no previous experience of testing, confident enough to take the next steps on your learning pathway in this field. The basic advice given in this book will point the way ahead. You could be introducing psychometric tests to your organization sooner than you think!

Fact-check (answers at back)

1. What options does an organization have if it has no qualified staff to administer and interpret psychometric tests?
   a) Use expert advice ❏
   b) Use a bureau service ❏
   c) Hope for the best ❏
   d) Develop in-house expertise ❏

2. To gain the required level of competence in using tests, which of these are among the areas in which will you need expertise?
   a) Selecting, administering and scoring tests ❏
   b) Interpreting the results ❏
   c) Collecting paperclips ❏
   d) Presenting complex information ❏

3. Is access to psychometric test materials in the UK restricted to those who are suitably qualified?
   a) Yes ❏
   b) No ❏
   c) Not yet ❏
   d) Mostly ❏

4. Which UK organization offers recognized qualifications in occupational testing?
   a) British Pharmaceutical Society ❏
   b) British Pharmacological Society ❏
   c) British Phycological Society ❏
   d) British Psychological Society ❏

5. What issues are relevant to the ethical use of tests?
   a) Communication ❏
   b) Candidate care ❏
   c) Equal opportunities ❏
   d) Culture fairness ❏

6. What steps can you take to promote equal opportunities?
   a) Evaluate the tests ❏
   b) Tell all the test-takers to wear the same clothes ❏
   c) Review the performance of test-takers ❏
   d) Modify the test administration if necessary ❏

7. What are the ideal conditions for locations used for testing?
   a) Quiet ❏
   b) Well illuminated ❏
   c) Soothing background music ❏
   d) Well ventilated ❏

8. What will happen if a test is interrupted or not administered properly?
   a) The results will still be valid ❏
   b) The results will still be valid if nobody says anything ❏
   c) The results will be invalid ❏
   d) The police will have to be called ❏

9. What measures should be in place with regard to the storing of test materials?
a) Locked storage facilities ☐
b) Unrestricted access ☐
c) Restricted access ☐
d) Company policies governing security and access ☐

10. What legislation is pertinent to the storage of test results?
a) Freedom of Information Act 2000 ☐
b) Health and Safety at Work Act 1974 ☐
c) Data Protection Act 1998 ☐
d) Official Secrets Act 1989 ☐

Surviving in tough times

In a difficult economic climate, the proven benefits of psychometric tests can be even more valuable. We've compiled a list of ten top tips – made up of key points worth repeating along with some fresh ideas for you to think about – to help you make the most of what testing has to offer when times are hard.

1 Don't skimp on research

Despite the economic downturn, resist the pressure to cut corners when researching which kind of tests to use in your organization. It will take time and resources to select the right test that matches your needs. This should be a rigorous exercise involving consulting experts and experienced users as well as an in-depth review of all the information available in print and online. Any money you think you will save by not investing in research could be greatly outweighed by the cost of implementing a testing regime that proves to be ineffective.

2 Shop around

There are many test publishers out there who are hungry for your business. Be a savvy buyer and look around to get the best deal for your organization. But don't be tempted to just go for the cheapest; that's rarely the best option. Instead, draw up a shortlist of publishers that can provide tests appropriate to your requirements. To do this, ask suppliers to show you samples of questionnaires, instructions, answer sheets and manuals. Ask them to provide references. Then find out if the association for your trade or profession can recommend anybody, and don't forget to consult reviews from independent sources such as the British Psychological Society. Once you've whittled down your shortlist to, say, three or four companies, then you can talk to them about price. And don't be afraid to negotiate!

3 Take ownership

Since tests need to be administered and interpreted by experts, you can be forgiven for thinking that it would be cheaper and easier to buy in outside expertise. After all, there are plenty suppliers out there to choose from. But this may not always be the best option. Investing in the development of in-house expertise, though costly in the short term, could put you in a better position in the long run. With your own qualified staff, your organization will be able to take ownership of the testing process, which will ensure that tests are always appropriate for the test-takers. Nobody will be better at identifying your target population than your own people.

4 Use tests for screening

With unemployment at high levels, an organization could be inundated with hundreds of job applications when advertising for a position. If you find yourself in that situation, you might think you can't see the wood for the trees. Where do you start? Well, psychometric tests offer a quick and relatively inexpensive method of eliminating large numbers of unsuitable candidates without resorting to initial screening interviews. The data gathered from testing can screen out candidates, helping you to draw up a shortlist of suitable applicants, and saving your HR department valuable time and resources.

5 Remember, tests are more than recruitment tools

Psychometric tests can offer far wider benefits to your organization than simply as an aid to recruiting new people. With recruitment freezes affecting many organizations in both the public and private sectors, testing will help you to make the most of the people you've already got. For instance, psychometric data can be used to select people for promotion, identify skills gaps by highlighting the personal development needs of individuals, coach members of your senior management team, and discover why staff are underperforming. It can also prove invaluable when putting teams together and for reducing the potential for conflict in the workplace, particularly at times of change, such as during a takeover or merger.

6 Don't rely on tests alone

Psychometric tests are relatively cheap but they should not be used in isolation. In this book we have discussed the drawbacks of traditional assessment methods, such as the application form, CV, references and job interview. We all remember a candidate who shined at the interview but turned out to be completely hopeless once appointed to the job. So long as you are fully aware of their shortcomings, these methods still have a role in the selection process. Tests by themselves will give you only part of the picture. But if you use them in conjunction with the other methods, you can considerably reduce the chances of making a costly mistake.

7 You don't have to be a big company to use tests

Today around 70 per cent of UK companies with more than 50 employees rely on psychometric tests, but that doesn't mean small and medium-sized businesses (SMEs) can't use them as well. In the early days of testing, the costs of the necessary training and materials were prohibitive and beyond the reach of most SMEs. However, growing competition in the marketplace means testing is now far more affordable. And it can be argued that a small family business has a greater need to use this tool than a large multinational, as the consequences of making the wrong appointment can be far more damaging, especially in a challenging economic environment.

8 Capitalize on testing's flexibility

It's a competitive world and constantly evolving. As a result, organizations have to be able to adapt to changing market conditions and meet demands for innovative products and services. This also means that established job roles have to change and organizations need to look for people with the right combination of skills that meet the new requirements for these roles. The inherent flexibility of testing allows you to identify the critical qualities required for a newly created job or specific function quite easily, allowing you to respond quickly to new demands from customers in the marketplace and maintain your competitiveness.

9 The shortcomings of formal qualifications

Another consequence of increasing competitiveness, together with globalization and the emergence of new economies, is that traditional academic qualifications in some quarters are no longer seen as relevant. Employers in a wide range of business and industry sectors have complained that school curricula and even university degree courses do not equip candidates with the skills and knowledge they need in the modern workplace. In a crowded job market, psychometric tests can be a better guide to finding those applicants with the abilities and attributes required.

10 Testing improves your credibility

As we have seen, one of the factors behind the growing use of psychometric testing in recent years has been the increasing professionalization of the Human Resources function. The scientific objectivity offered by testing is in keeping with a more sophisticated approach to recruitment, which has previously been regarded as being a highly subjective process. Thus, organizations that employ psychometrics can improve their standing and credibility – in the eyes of customers, suppliers, stakeholders and would-be employees – by being seen as modern, professional and promoting equal opportunities.

Answers

Sunday: 1b; 2c; 3a, b, c & d;
4a, b & c; 5b, c & d; 6a, b & c;
7d; 8a, b, c & d; 9c; 10c
Monday: 1a & c; 2b, c & d; 3b; 4a,
b & d; 5a, b & d; 6 None, they
all are; 7c; 8c; 9c;
10a & c
Tuesday: 1c; 2a, b, c & d; 3b; 4a,
b & d; 5c; 6c; 7b; 8a, b & d; 9d;
10c
Wednesday: 1d; 2c; 3c; 4c;
5b; 6b & c; 7b; 8a, b & d; 9c &
d; 10a, c & d

Thursday: 1d; 2b; 3c; 4d;
5c; 6a, b, c & d; 7c; 8b;
9a, b, c & d; 10a, b & d
Friday: 1a, b & d; 2a, b & c;
3c; 4a, b & d; 5c; 6b;
7b & c; 8a, b, c & d; 9b & d;
10a, c & d
Saturday: 1a, b & d; 2a, b & d;
3a; 4d; 5a, b, c & d;
6a, c & d; 7a, b & d; 8c;
9a, c & d; 10c

Useful contacts

Organizations

The British Psychological Society (BPS)
48 Princess Road East, Leicester LE1 7DR
Tel.: 0116 254 9568, Fax: 0116 247 0787
www.bps.org.uk

Chartered Management Institute
Management House, Cottingham Road,
Corby, Northants, NN17 1TT
Tel.: 01536 204222
www.managers.org.uk

**The Chartered Institute of Personnel
and Development (IPD)**
151 The Broadway, London SW19 1JQ
Tel.: 020 8612 6200
www.cipd.org.uk

Test suppliers and publishers

Oxford Psychologists Press Ltd
Elsfield Hall
15–17 Elsfield Way, Oxford OX2 8EP
Tel.: 0845 6039958
www.opp.co.uk

Psytech International Ltd
The Grange, Church Road, Pulloxhill, Beds, MK45 5HE
Tel.: 01525 720003
www.psytech.co.uk

SHL Group
The Pavilion, 1 Atwell Place Thames Ditton, Surrey, KT7 0NE
Tel.: 020 8398 4170
www.shldirect.com

Further reading

BPS (1989) *Psychological Testing: Guidance for the User*, Leicester: The British Psychological Society.

Cherniss, C. & Goleman, D. (2001) *The Emotionally Intelligent Workplace. How to Select for, Measure and Improve Emotional Intelligence in Individuals, Groups, and Organizations*, Jossey-Bass, San Francisco.

EOC (1988) *Avoiding Sex Bias in Selection Testing: Guidance for Employers*, Manchester: Equal Opportunities Commission.

Gael S. (1987) *The Job Analysis Handbook for Business, Industry and Government*, Chichester: John Wiley & Sons.

Goleman, D. (1995) *Emotional Intelligence*, Bantam, NY.

IPD (1993) *The IPM Code on Psychological Testing*, London: The Institute of Personnel and Development.

Pearn, M. & Kandola, R. (1988) *Job Analysis – A Practical Guide for Managers*, London: The Institute of Personnel Management – now IPD.

Smith, M. & Robertson, I. (1993) *Advances in Selection and Assessment*, Chichester: John Wiley & Sons.

Useful web pages

www.pantesting.com – web-based test supplier.
www.eiconsortium.org – the official site for the Consortium for Research on Emotional Intelligence, which contains many articles and some case studies on the subject.

Notes

ALSO AVAILABLE IN THE 'IN A WEEK' SERIES

BODY LANGUAGE FOR MANAGEMENT • BOOKKEEPING AND
ACCOUNTING • CUSTOMER CARE • SPEED READING • DEALING WITH
DIFFICULT PEOPLE • EMOTIONAL INTELLIGENCE • FINANCE FOR
NON-FINANCIAL MANAGERS • INTRODUCING MANAGEMENT
• MANAGING YOUR BOSS • MARKET RESEARCH • NEURO-LINGUISTIC
PROGRAMMING • OUTSTANDING CREATIVITY • PLANNING YOUR
CAREER • SUCCEEDING AT INTERVIEWS • SUCCESSFUL APPRAISALS
• SUCCESSFUL ASSERTIVENESS • SUCCESSFUL BUSINESS PLANS
• SUCCESSFUL CHANGE MANAGEMENT • SUCCESSFUL COACHING
• SUCCESSFUL COPYWRITING • SUCCESSFUL CVS • SUCCESSFUL
INTERVIEWING

For information about other titles
in the series, please visit
www.inaweek.co.uk

ALSO AVAILABLE IN THE 'IN A WEEK' SERIES

For information about other titles
in the series, please visit
www.inaweek.co.uk

LEARN IN A WEEK, WHAT THE EXPERTS LEARN IN A LIFETIME

For information about other titles in the series, please visit www.inaweek.co.uk